DETOURS OF LIFE

JAMI BAUER

Copyright © 2023 Jami Bauer

Paperback: 978-1-962256-99-5
eBook: 978-1-962256-98-8
Library of Congress Control Number: 2023914763

All rights reserved. No part of this publication may be reproduced, distributed, or transmitted in any form or by any electronic or mechanical means, without the prior written permission of the publisher, except in the case of brief quotations embodied in critical reviews and certain other noncommercial uses permitted by copyright law.

Ordering Information:

BookTrail Agency
8838 Sleepy Hollow Rd.
Kansas City, MO 64114

Printed in the United States of America

Contents

Sanctuary 1
Stereotype 3
Eternal Sleep 5
In Nature 7
If I Could 9
Detours of Life 11
Inner Climate 13
Which Way 15
Wish upon a Star 17
Within Reach 19
Detrimental Demand 21
Self-Analysis 23
What's the Meaning? 25
Simple Pleasures 27
Jigsaw Puzzle 29
Trial and Error 31
Carry Yourself 33
Self-Belief 35
Beginning with the End 37
Perseverance 39
Jumping to Conclusions 41
No Rush 43
New Day Tomorrow 45
Don't Make Me 47

Scattered	49
Eclipse	51
Let Me Be Me	53
Emotional Cruise	55
Overcast Inside	57
As a Child	59
I'm Not to Know	61
Humor Me	63
Definition of a Friend	65
Beyond Words	67
It's Late	69
Smile over Frowns	71
Life	73
Never Alone	75
Adaptations	77
The Holes Have Made Me Whole	79
Absence So Present	81
The Best Thing	83
The Shell	85
Who's There?	87
Just for a Day	89
Today	91
In Awe	93
Only So Much	95
This Life	97
Quietude of My Solitude	99
About the Author	101

To my family and friends
and in loving memory of my dad,
Dr. Bruce Bauer.

Special thanks to my mentor,
friend and poet
Laureate Carol Connolly.

Sanctuary

Silence within me
in a world that screams.

Calmness like a lake in the early morning,
glasslike,
peaceful,
tranquil.

The energy on reserve awaiting
me, wanting to help,
eager.

Trust, and endless stability
to help keep my sanity.

I travel to my inner sanctuary
to find these commodities.
They are all free
within
me.

Stereotype

They don't even know you,
yet they call you by name.
You see, it's quite simple—
it's a societal game.
They can't see what's within
because they are living without.
They'll be quick to put a
label on you, without a doubt.
It's an easy alibi yet such a shame.
They don't even know you,
yet they call you by name.

Eternal Sleep

You lie asleep,
not only today
but for eternity.
I have wished many times
you would awaken.
We sleep as you do,
and in the night, we dream of you,
and during the day,
we think of you.
You lie asleep
but are always
awake
in our minds.

In Nature

In nature, all things are real.
I begin to feel
worries drift away with the river's current.
My spirit is cleansed
by the wondrous waterfalls.
The bright yellow butterflies with black dots on their wings
remind me of natural beauty, change, growth,
life, and death.
The huge rocks and towering trees remind me of our smallness
and their power. They've been here
hundreds of years.
I feel their wisdom and absorb their strength.
The seagulls teach me to take things lightly, sing, and see things
from a different view.
In nature, all things are real.
In nature, I learn,
I feel,
I am.

If I Could

If I could take away the pain you feel,
believe me, it would be gone.

If I could create more happiness instead of sorrow,
it would be created by tomorrow.

If I could jump inside and instill self-pride,
you'd be so proud of you and me.

If I could do all these things,
believe me, they would be done.

Detours of Life

𝒟riving ahead toward our goals,
the path appears clear—a sense of control.
Ahead in the distance, an unplanned design,
envisioning smooth roads on the highway of life—
what pleasant thoughts to possess.
Are the roads ever that nice?
They are not always smooth or free of construction.
We must come to realize this to avoid self-destruction.
There are often roadblocks, potholes, yield signs,
and other deviations.
These challenges help us reach our souls' destinations.
These detours of life may seem like burdens.
The construction is done for a purpose—to repair or make it better.
Drive through the detours with a sense of creation.
Keep moving forward toward your life's destination.
You'll see that these setbacks will help you survive,
for they are only temporary roadblocks
on the highway of life.

Inner Climate

*W*e choose our attitude, which
leads to our actions or inactions.
Adjustment of one's inner climate is a daily task.
Finding the right balance
can be a daily victory if chosen wisely
or defeat if chosen with haste.
When inspiration and motivation encompass your
mind, it feels like the warm sun shining on
your face, creating smiles and glorious wonder.
We all can choose
our inner climate, our forecast for the day.
So, tell the truth: What would your ideal weather be if you
were giving the forecast in your mind?
We all know people who choose to forecast rain,
hail, and thunderstorms
and others who choose to forecast sunshine,
clear skies, and light breezes to warm themselves and
others around them.
You choose your inner weather,
your inner climate,
so choose wisely and with care.
Choose to forecast sunshine, warmth, and blue skies.
Choose happiness.

Which Way

*W*hich way will you choose to use
your eyes,
your information,
your perceptions?

So many different ways to see one thing.

Will you choose drama,
pain,
misery,
poor me?

Or

will you choose
humor, perspective,
reflection,
rich me?

Which one will it be?

Wish upon a Star

*A*s I stared up at the mystic night sky,
I lost myself in thoughts of you,
wondering if you were happy and singing in heaven.
The illumination of the full moon
mesmerized my mind, body, and soul.
I suddenly felt you near. I wished upon a star you'd appear.
Although you've gone on your journey far from home,
you'll live, breathe, and sing in my heart forever.
You left this earth in such a rush, a haze, a blur,
no time for a last hug, cry, or goodbye.
You disappeared, stopping your breath and life on earth.
Your departure was not in the plans, not a choice—
no forewarning of your unfortunate fate that day.
Although you've gone on your journey so far away from home,
you will live, breathe, and sing in my heart forever.

Within Reach

𝒲ithin reach
(but never a grasp).

Wanting so much
(but afraid to ask).

Expecting too much
(high expectations).

Downgrading abilities
(setting limitations).

Unlock the cuffs
(free your hands),

for you
to hold
the key.

Detrimental Demand

We are hard on ourselves,
expecting too much in an unreliable world—
tough on our souls in fear of never
reaching our goals,
unneeded pressure in an unrealistic society,
striving to achieve everything
yet feeling we've accomplished nothing.
Why are we so hard on ourselves?
Feelings of inadequacies fill our brains
while feeling at times we're going insane.
Why is it we are so hard on ourselves?
Trying to fill every need
without giving in to societal greed,
can we ever be satisfied by the
way we are classified?
It's time to get a grasp of what we
can realistically achieve.
It's time to stop doubting and just
believe.

Self-Analysis

Take a look at yourself with your own eyes
instead of with those eyes that are not yours.

Compare yourself to the person in the mirror
instead of to those neither close nor dear.

Live for yourself, not for others.
Give kindly to your soul,
and then
speak the truth.

Love,
Yourself

What's the Meaning?

To strive, grasp, and hold on to all that you can,
and appreciate the life that has been given to
you.
So much is said, and so little is done.
When do we begin to live?
Don't walk in others' shadows, for that
will only keep you in the dark.
Do laugh a lot, for laughter is a gift for
happiness and wellness.
Open your wings in the course of life,
for if you keep them closed,
you shall recede until one day,
you crash and dwindle away.
Be thankful for your strong qualities,
and learn from your mistakes.
So what is the meaning?
It's all within you and all that you do.

Simple Pleasures

A whole day goes by, and the next
is on its way.
What did you do and learn today?
Did you learn to laugh when your job is too much to bear?
Did you learn to compliment someone
or just show that you care?
Did you stop to feel love
in a world so full of hate?
Did you learn from a friend, child, or mate?
The fact is we are learning so much each day.
It's like an ongoing course,
with no credits or cost.
The truth is we must learn each day,
or else we'll be lost.

Love,
Still Learning

Jigsaw Puzzle

It's the end of the day.
Lying in bed,
analyzing what's been done and said,
trying to put life into perspective
is a daily chore.
Some days are harder to bear.

It's a giant jigsaw puzzle,
with many pieces, shapes, and
colors.
Trying to piece together to create a whole,
sometimes the pieces don't fit
no matter how hard we try,
and we realize that others fit better.

Similar to the misfits are the mistakes we make in life.
With patience, persistence, and
perspective, we can piece it together
in time.

Trial and Error

How do we know if we're not willing to try?
How can we live in fear for our lives?
So often we feel so uncertain, like we might even fail.
We feel so timid, so rigid, and so frail.
We must be willing to let down our guards
and allow things to happen without trying so
hard.
We must reach forward and look beyond the terror.
We must live and learn through trial and error.
Push forward, look ahead, and breakthrough life's many barriers—
that will take courage and strength
and many trials and errors.

Love,
Only Human

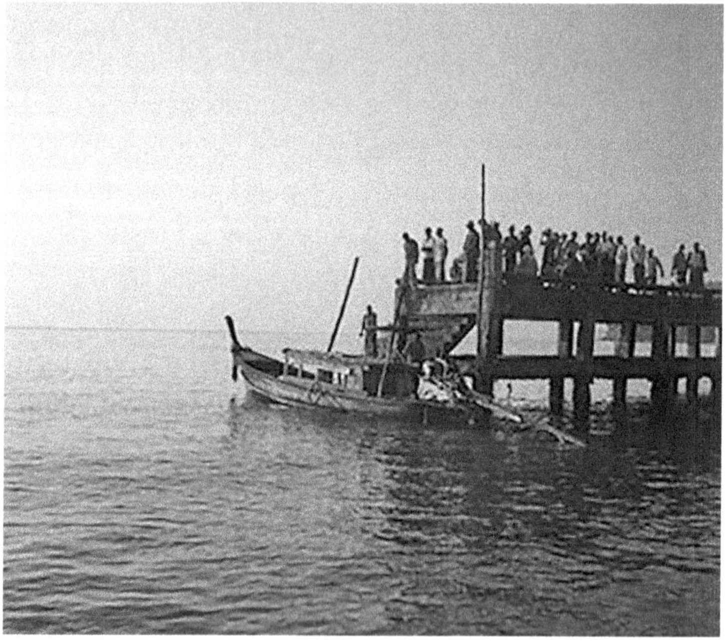

Carry Yourself

Your talent can only carry you so far.
After that, you carry yourself.
Whatever you do has been done before.
That's why you have to give just a little more.
Doors will open as they will close.
Take your openings, and fly away.
People will put you up, just as they
will bring you down. Rise to the occasion,
and smile over the frowns.
You can if you believe. No one can
steal that or make you mean.
If you choose to be a success, then the world
is at your mercy.
If you choose to fail, then the world
is a thousand enemies.
You can if you will and will if you can.
Your talent can only carry you so far.
After that, you carry yourself.

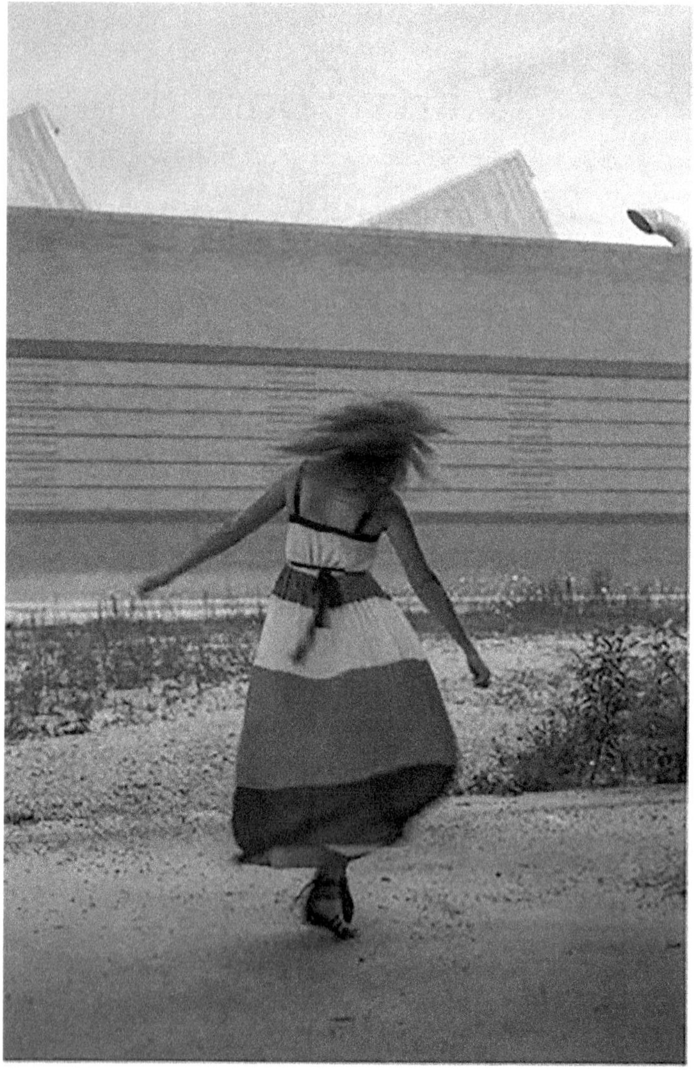

Self-Belief

One heart, one soul, an ever-striving
individual with many goals,
so much talent and support,
many who believe in you and the various
things you pursue—
is that enough to carry you through?
To have friends, family, and believers
is just one facet of your make.
It's all quite simple yet so complex.
What does it really take?
It starts within. It starts with you
and ends with you.
It's a realization of reality and dreams.
It all starts with self-belief.

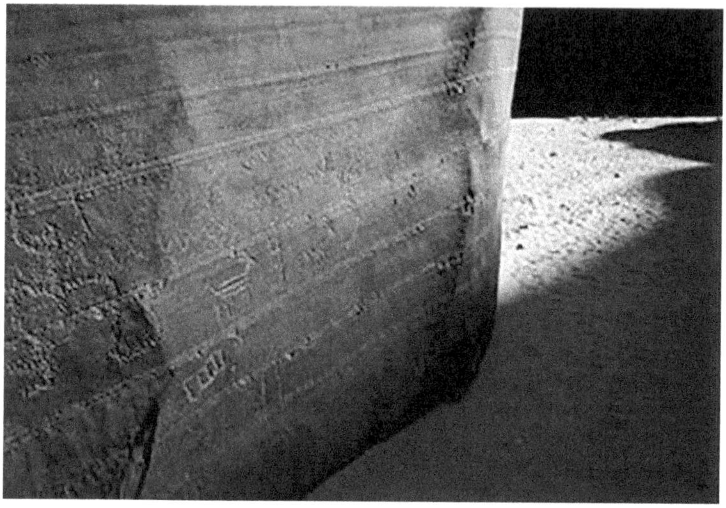

Beginning with the End

Create in your mind a crystal-clear vision of who and
what you want to become, not what others want you to be.
It's your journey, life, and pride, not something for others to decide;
begin living with the end in mind.
Don't dwell on what used to be, but delight in what could and can be.
We are such a seeking society, thinking that our ship will sail safely to shore.
Only with wise guidance and goals will the ship endure;
begin living with the end in mind.
Create as an artist would, and paint a picture in your
mind of who and what you desire to be.
Don't be a message in a bottle randomly thrown out to sea.
You are the captain of your own destiny;
begin living with the end in mind.
Let your soul be your sail and your heart's passion be the
wind, and your mind will guide you on your journey.
Let your true desires, dreams, and goals surface to be
the fuel for the fire, your joy and your purpose.
Don't let external obstacles destroy your inner passion,
but let them strengthen you for a better view;
it's time to begin living with the end in mind.
Your being needs a guide just as a symphony needs a conductor.
Be the professor of your own class, your favorite instructor;
begin living with the end in mind.
Paint a picture, and sculpt your thoughts
for success and happiness.
Be the Picasso of painting, the reason for the rhyme,
the strong oak tree grown from a tiny seed.
Use all the colors, tools, visions, and dreams to create a masterpiece.
Begin now with courage and strength, and visualize your time;
begin living with the end in mind.

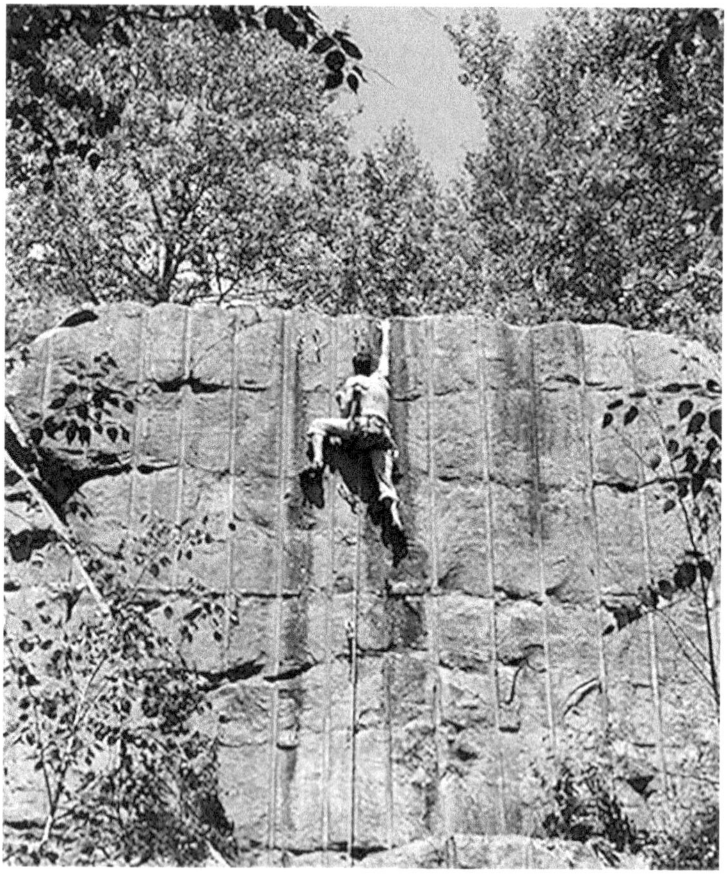

Perseverance

What is it when you've been knocked down
not once or twice
but again and again and again . . .
then once more?
Do you stay where you lay or stand up,
wipe off the dirt, patch the wounds,
walk forward knowing the more
you've been knocked down,
the stronger you grow,
the more you learn.
You continue to walk proud . . . you persevere.
What is it when you've been told,
"No way, never, you can't"?
You hold your chin up high and say with pride,
"I can; I will. The challenge is my friend,
my companion till the end."
What is it when you have a dream so grand and wondrous
that you decide to journey toward it?
You achieve your heart's desire—
a small idea, then a big idea, then goals,
and then a dream come true.
What is it when you can do anything you
put your mind to while others say you cannot?
That's perseverance!

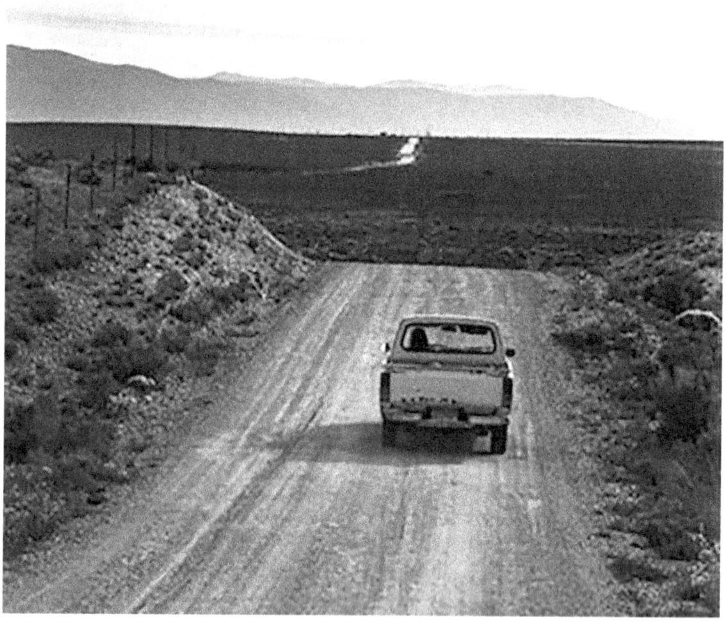

Jumping to Conclusions

It seems as though we jump to conclusions
to find life solutions.
It is not the answer nor the route to take;
it is a jovial journey we make.
Through different roads and diverse relations,
we learn the explanation of our existence
and our purpose.
With patience and persistence,
not the poison of false predictions,
we learn the art and essence of living.
It seems as though we jump to conclusions
to find the solutions to life.
It's like life is an ongoing novel, a best-selling book,
so good it's hard to put down—
so fascinating you want to share pages with others.
So why jump to the ending
when the journey, each page, encompasses the meaning,
the unfolding, beauty, and truth.
It seems as though we jump to conclusions
to find solutions to life
instead of enjoying the journey,
trusting in life;
in now, our higher power,
ourselves.

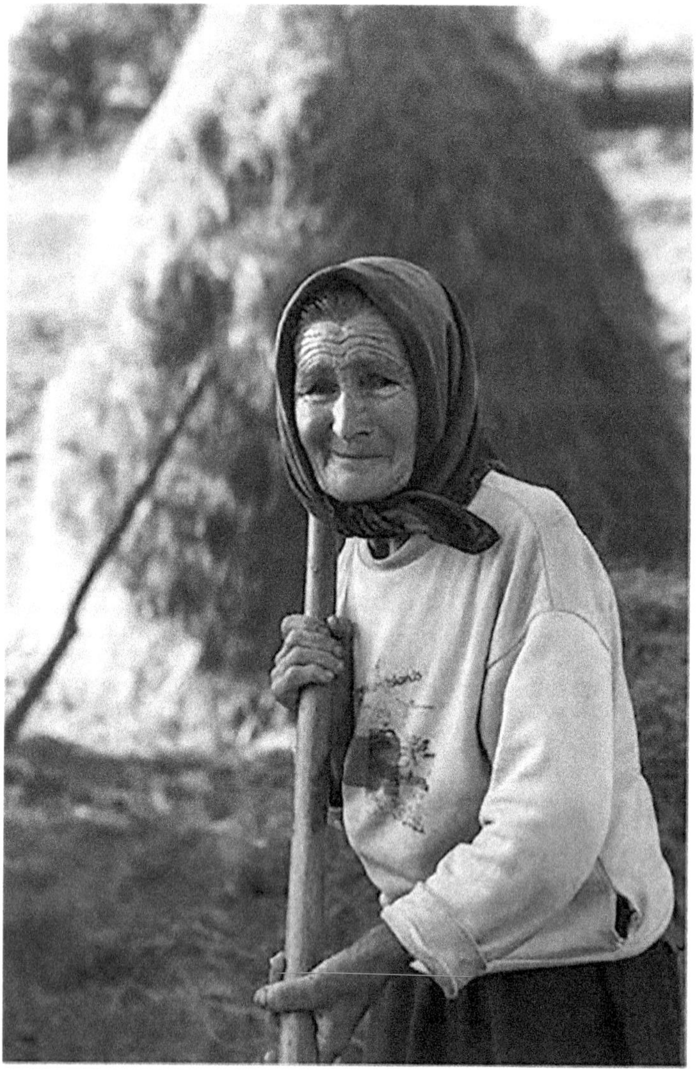

No Rush

Just a bit more time, and we will be just fine.
We have to begin, reach within . . . find patience.
When things don't go quite your way,
don't get tense and shout out loud.
Just hush; there's no rush.
To expect perfectionism is to jump into the fire.
To understand adversity is to be friends with the flame.
So sit back and count on what you can control:
yourself, your attitude, and your inner world.

Love,
Patience

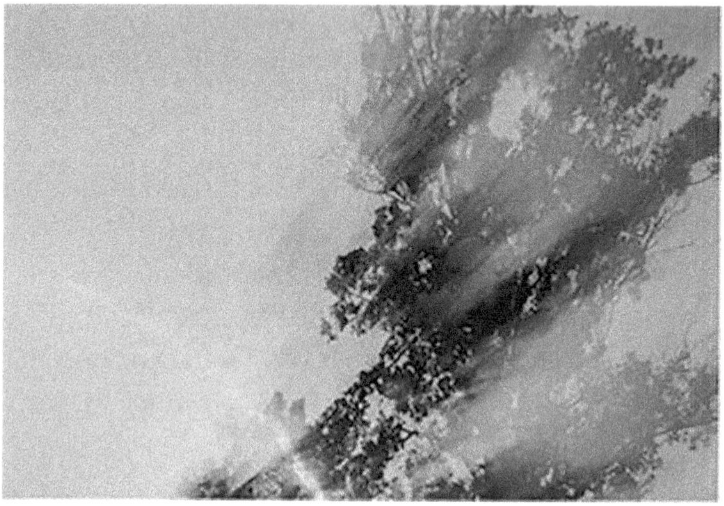

New Day Tomorrow

New day tomorrow,
wipe away this sorrow;
clear my slate.

Dry the tears,
burn the fears,
watch the smoke rise.

Is love so brittle,
snapping like a tree's branch
in a winter storm,

or does the storm create strength?

New day tomorrow,
wipe away this sorrow;
clear my slate.

Renew my faith in people,
in possibilities,
that love can survive any storm.

In love, all is possible . . .

In hate, all dies.

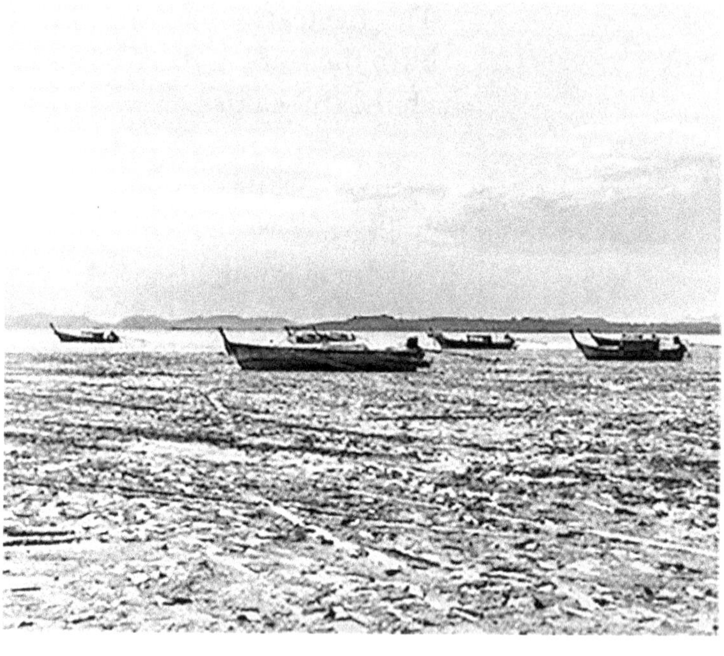

Don't Make Me

Don't make me the source of your sorrows
or the outlet for your rage.

Your emotions should not be outwardly directed,
but rather inwardly reflected,
for if there is a hostile flame burning inside you,
it should be maintained, tended to . . . eventually put to rest.

Don't make me the center of your sadness,
nor the witness of your badness,
for it's not me you should try to hurt;
it's you
you should mend.

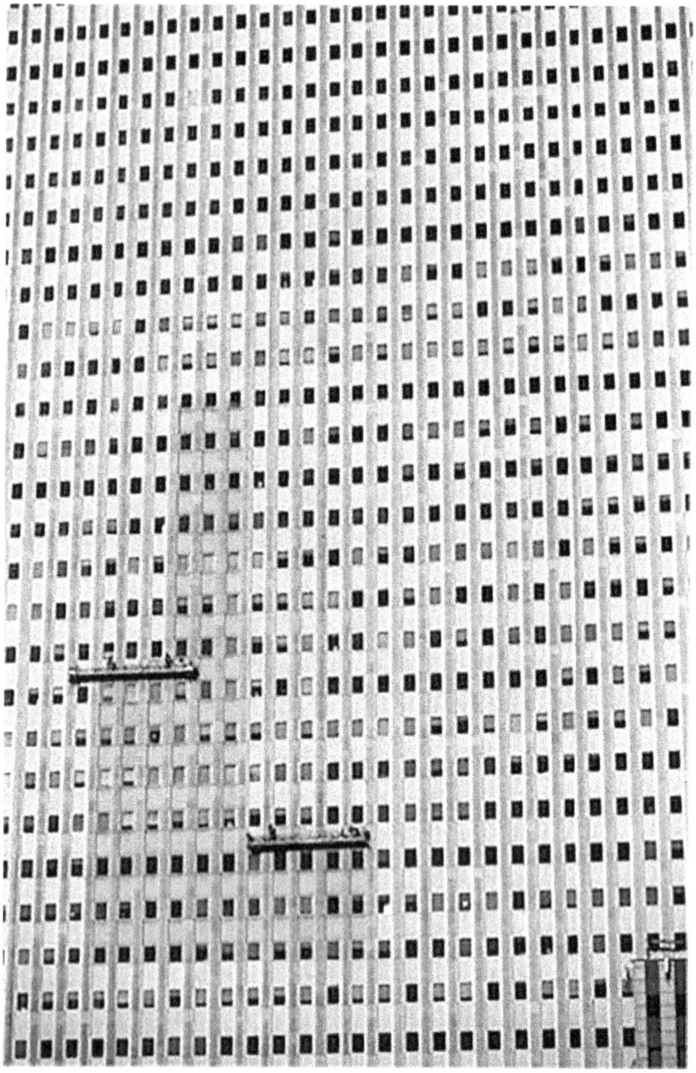

Scattered

Here I am, so focused and so driven.
Now I lose my focus and my vision.
Where did they go, once prominent in my mind?
Who is to tell if it's of the scattered kind?
My goals are many, my expectations
high. I feel self-assured completeness,
and pride.
What a shame these feelings come and go.
When they will stay for good, I'm not to know.
Scattered are my thoughts, my visions, and my dreams.
Are they really so tangled? Or so it seems.
It seems we are all reaching for stability in such an unstable world.
It seems to me our lives are all quite scattered.

૭

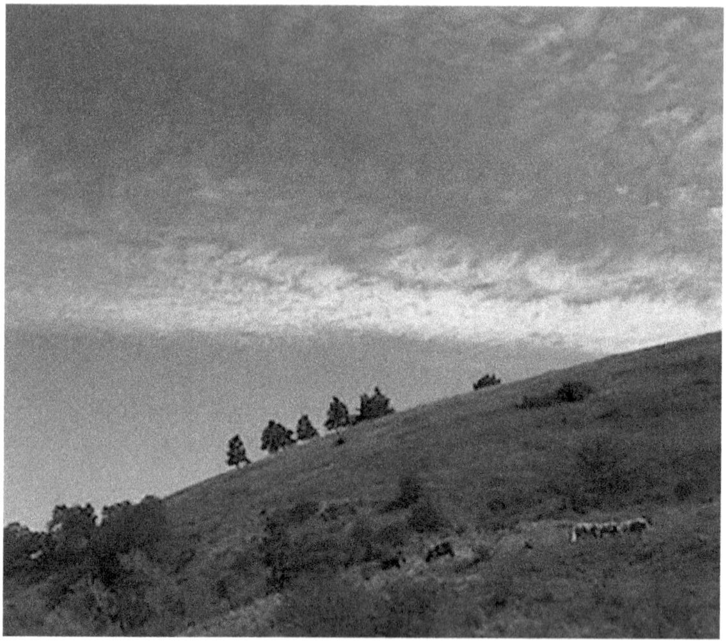

Eclipse

If you don't see the sunshine on my face today,
it doesn't mean it is lost forever.
It will be found on another day.
I've had a lot of things happen around and to me;
the clouds have covered up the sun but only temporarily.
I have faith that the sun will make its way
through the clouds again.
Sunshine is one of my very dear friends. If
you don't see the glow on my face today,
it doesn't mean it is lost forever.
It can be found again on another day.
I've been through enough storms to know that
the bad weather will pass,
yet it is sometimes hard to predict
when it will hit.
I know that
after the storm,
I'll see the colorful rainbow
with its arch of hope and happiness.
If you don't see the sunshine
on my face today,
it doesn't mean it is lost forever.
It will be found again
on another day.

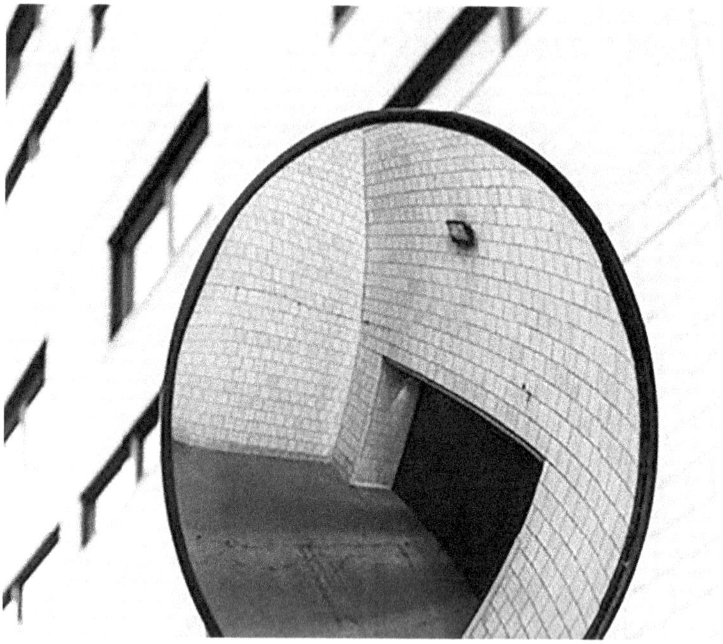

Let Me Be Me

When people begin to tell me what I
should think and how I must feel,
I begin to feel mechanical
and a part of me not real,
for I am solely human,
doing the best I can.
Deep emotions in my mind—
they need to be expressed,
or else they grow unkind.
Similar to a prisoner locked up and isolated
are my feelings.
Acceptance can
free my uncertainties,
and create expression for my
repressions. My spirit is strong; my
roots deep.
So please let me be me,
feel what I feel,
and think what I think.

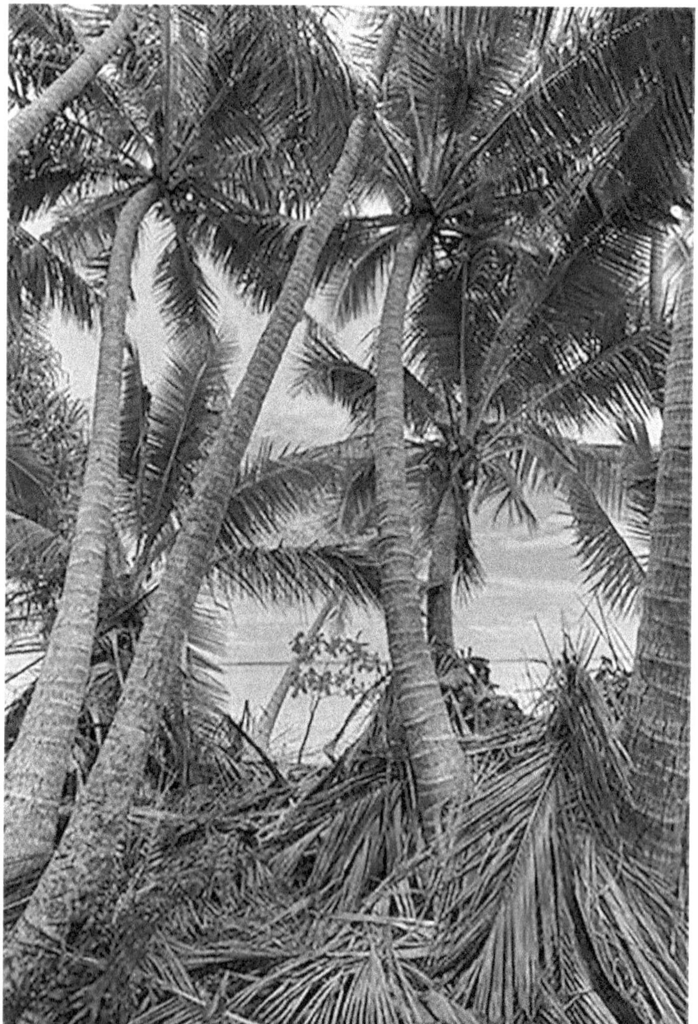

Emotional Cruise

I sent my emotions on a summer cruise; you see, they've been working overtime.
It's like trying to run a marathon each day for thirty days in a row: exhausting, depletion of total energy (mind and body).
They never complained; it just seemed like all they did was train, race, and then race some more.
Constant thinking, constant running, constant emotions—
it's like trying to take an essay exam on each area of life
each day for twelve hours in a row.
No breaks, no fluids, no food—just work, think, write, and then work some more.
This is what the emotions feel like—overworked and underpaid.
Many times, their hard labor goes unnoticed—no recognition, not even a simple thanks. This is why I had no hesitation nor reservation when they came to me ever so softly, so tired, worn down, looking like a savage after a day in one-hundred-degree heat in the desert sun without water or shade. I whispered to them in a kind voice and said, "You are free to go wherever you choose," I suggested a weeklong cruise.
They looked at me as a child being told they are going to the fair,
wide-eyed and animated and without a care in the world.
They were now free to frolic and have fun and get away from the constant hammering of life.
They could feel free and light like feathers floating on the sea.
The fifty-pound packs they carry on their backs can be left behind,
for they need no weight nor heaviness of thought.
They just need themselves; solitude; silence;
clean, crisp air;
clear blue skies; an abundance of truth, love, and understanding;
nature's music of waves and seagulls;
peacefulness; and soothing rest.
Bon voyage!

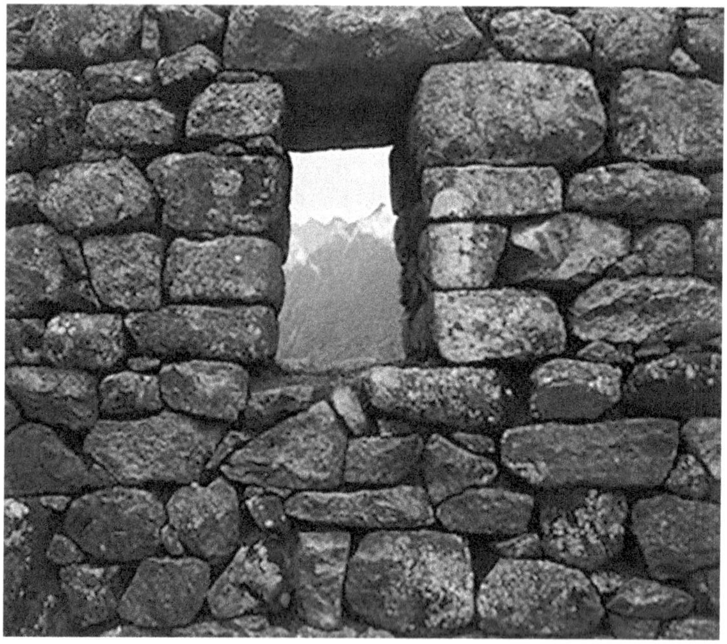

Overcast Inside

On days when the clouds seem to never end
when overcast sky haunts your being,
reach within to create your own sunshine.
Oh, but it is so easy to let the clouds darken our minds . . .
It takes a special human being to
bring lightness from within.

Love,
A ray of light

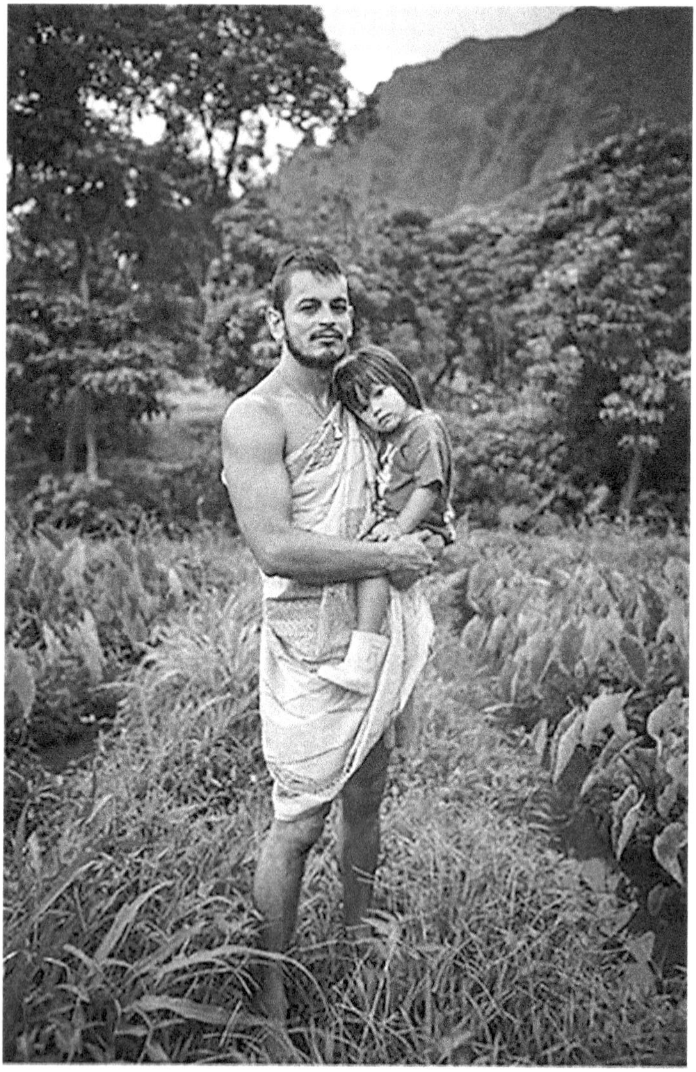

As a Child

A child does not think before hugging;
she just hugs.

A child does not think before loving;
she just loves.

A child does not see through tainted glasses;
her vision is crystal clear.

Next time you wonder how to think,
act, or be,
trust in your inner child;
she holds so much truth.

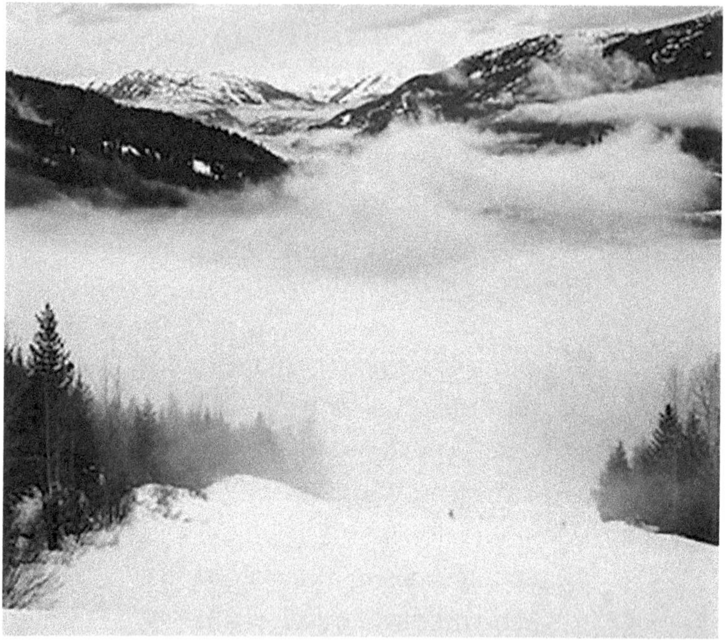

I'm Not to Know

You're not even gone, yet I'm missing you
and all that you are about.
I see you full of life today;
tomorrow, that could be stripped away.
I'm not to know.
I'm with you each day, holding your hand, rubbing your arms,
watching your eyes and the rise and fall of your chest.
I see you so full of life today;
tomorrow, that could be stripped away.
I'm not to know.
You squeeze my hand and give me a grin
even though it hurts in your body and bones;
you surface to celebrate for a while.
Surrounded by love,
today, you talk of tomorrow;
tomorrow, you may be gone.
I'm not to know.
Reliving memories, singing together,
crying inside as I cherish each moment,
I embrace each breath, for I see you so full of life today;
tomorrow, that could be stripped away.
I'm not to know.
I write about you now as I see your eyes and your chest rise and fall;
tomorrow, you may be gone,
and only heaven knows what tomorrow holds.

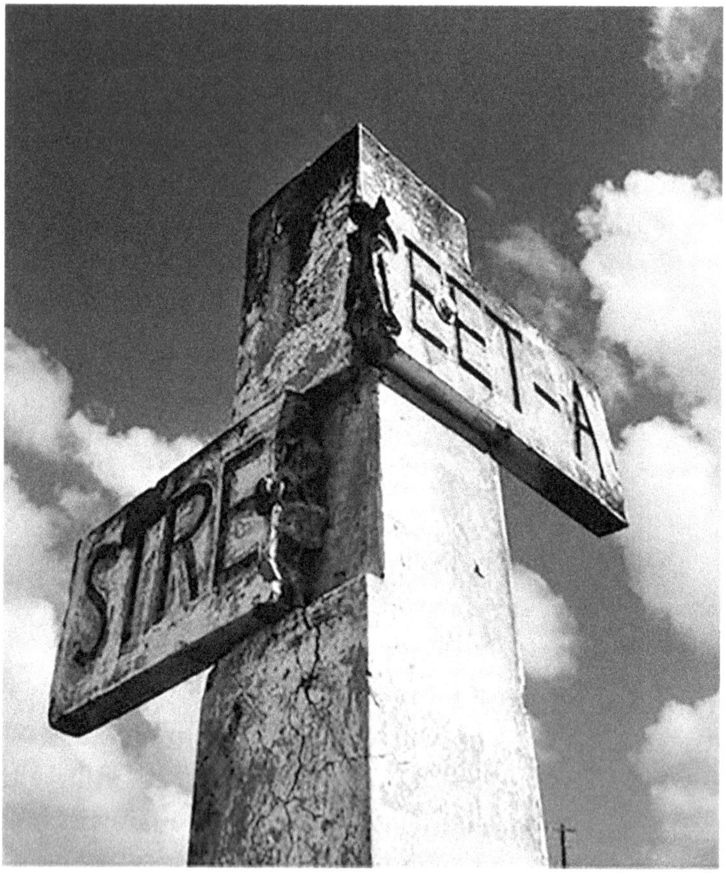
STRE
EET-A

Humor Me

What role does laughter play in your world?
When you lose your grin, you begin to lose the
fun that life has to offer.
When you've had a trying day and life
has put you on the burner, so hot and unbearable,
give yourself a smile, laugh, and jump into the cool pool.
This world is a daily challenge, and the biggest victory is if
you can laugh at and with yourself,
and then share your joy with the world.

HELLO
my name is
竹葉叶

Definition of a Friend

No dictionary could define what a friend is or
what one should be.
It's all self-defined; it comes from you and me.
If your definition is a one-way street,
what a pity we had to meet,
for friends travel on a two-way path,
supporting each other endlessly.
A friend is someone who cares when no
one else believes.
A friend shares needs, wants, desires, sorrow, and pain.
If these are not in your vocabulary,
what is there to gain?
Our definitions don't have to meet
but rather should mesh.
If they are not at all similar but skewed,
it's time to meet other friends.
It's time to start fresh.
No dictionary could define you or me.
We can be found in each other.

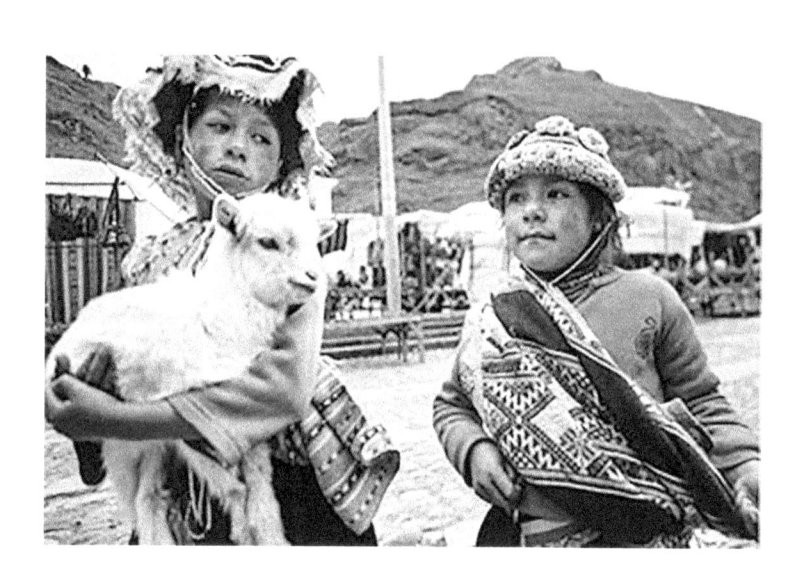

Beyond Words

There are so many channels through which to speak.
Your face and body tell me so much.
Your hurried walk with rigid posture
tells me you are upset, uptight;
something is not quite right.
Your eyes drifting off to sea
tell me there's something you are not sharing with me.
The sullen smile you struggle to make
tells me you've had a bad day.
Study a friend, child, or mate,
and without a word,
a story will be told, a message heard.
The conversation takes
place on the body and
face . . . beyond words.

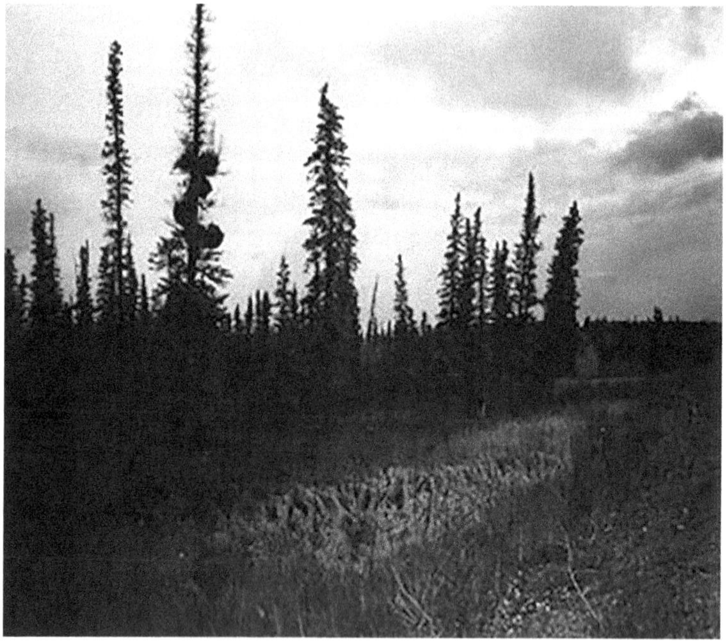

It's Late

It's late; I know I should be in bed,
but so much is awake inside my head.
I grab a book and read a page.
My thoughts override the words.
I shut the book.
Too much curiosity and so many unanswered questions—
I'm always wondering and my mind wondering.
I wish there was a button to press to quiet the riots
in my mind.
I know it's late; I should be in bed,
but so much is awake inside my head.
With one last look, I pick up the book.
I begin to read the line where I left off.
It simply says, "Go to bed; it's late!"

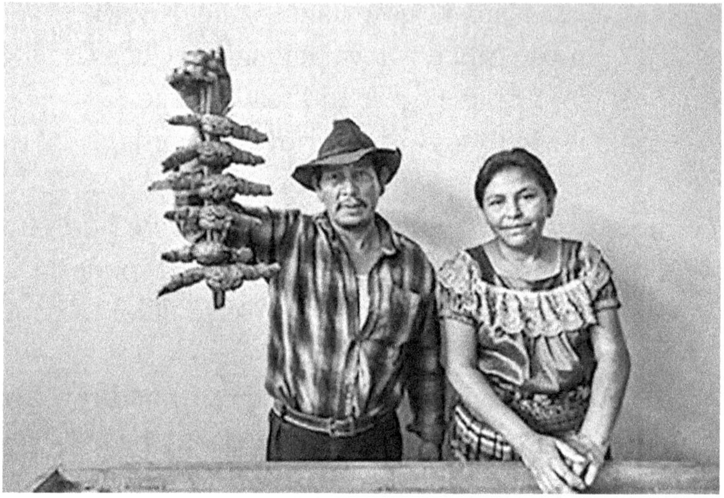

Smile over Frowns

When people try to bring you down,
just smile over the frowns.
People like to see you crumble,
just as a football team hopes for a fumble.
You have to be strong
when they try to convince you you're wrong.
Shield the false bearings and untruths,
and only let the reality of your soul shine through.
When people try to bring you down, take a deep breath,
and smile over the frowns.

Life

We live, we love, we learn . . . why do we have to mourn?
When someone we love has been taken above,
it is our love that is sent with them.
In our lives, we never do know just when it is our turn
to go,
so we live each day one by one as if our lives have just begun.
Every minute, every hour really should be treated like a delicate flower.
Like a rose that can bloom and grow, there is a chance that it will
close.
We will know the meaning of life as soon as life is taken away.
Some advice to you and me is to live our life like a tree—
planted and plotted and put on this earth
to bloom and grow from a beautiful birth.
Through wind, rain, sun, and snow, it stays alive
because it knows that it must lose its leaves
just as we must lose our loved ones.
Keep hope, joy, and love;
live each day like a new ray of light,
for we are blessed to live our lives.
Be yourself; that is all you must be.
Go through life living one day at a time, and you will live a life divine.
I wish, I hope, I pray for you
that you will live as long as you truly dream to.
Just reach out if you're in doubt,
for there is always someone to lend a hand.
First, love yourself and the miracle of life, and you will
respect both day and night.
That is where we should all start—
not far from reality
but close to Earth.

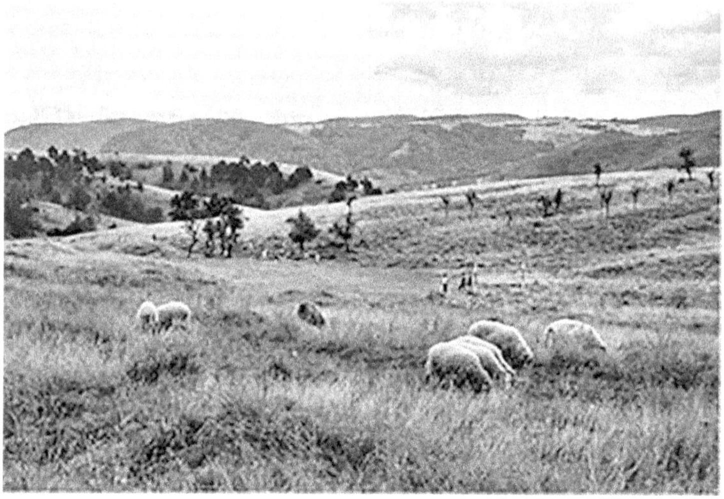

Never Alone

Never alone with the feelings you have—
only alone when you hide them deep inside.
Never alone with the fears you face—
only alone when you don't face your fears.
Never alone when you want to cry—
only sad when those tears don't dry.
Never alone when you think to yourself—
detrimental if those thoughts you oppress.
Next time you begin to feel isolated,
scared, or in disbelief,
know that others and I share these
thoughts you think.
Walk by yourself, but realize
you are never alone.

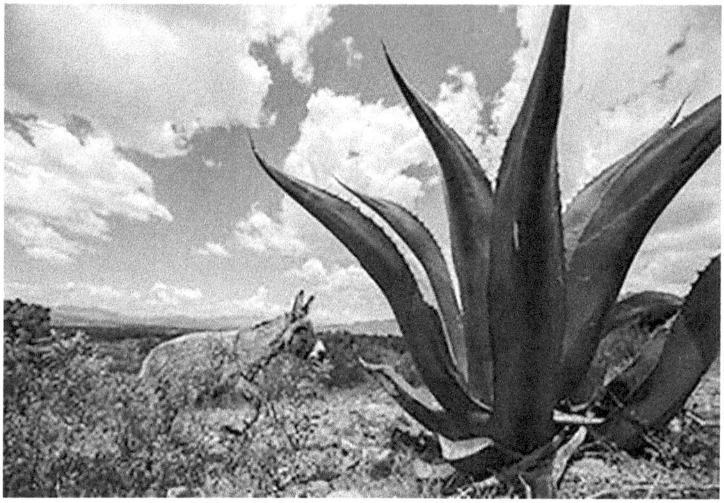

Adaptations

I'm always running here and there, facing
changes everywhere.
Different people,
odd places—I guess there are all forms of adaptations.
As soon as something starts to mesh, I have
to pack and start fresh.
You might expect I'd lose my grace.
I will continue, take things in stride,
take time, have patience . . .
This will mean more
adaptations.

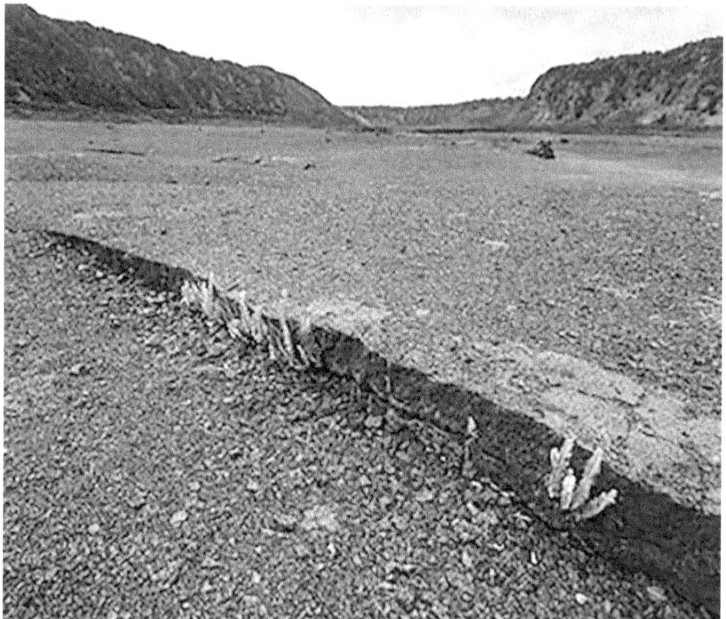

The Holes Have Made Me Whole

The holes in my life have made me whole.
When it seemed no one loved me, I loved myself.
When praise was nowhere to be found, I patted my own back.
When hurdles arose, I jumped everyone, increasing my strength.
The holes in my life have made me whole.
When no one sang with me, I sang a solo for the world to hear.
When concern was low and my flesh cold,
I warmed myself with an attitude of honor and ideas of love.
When I walked down the dark wooded path without a hand to hold,
I reached for my own hand; I nurtured my spirit, my inner soul.
When the phone stopped ringing and no messages were heard, I
called myself and wrote a letter to my soul.
It seems like the holes in my life have made me whole.
When empty promises were made,
I made a promise to myself.
When lies were whispered and rumors abounded,
I turned inward to shatter the false
and let the truth surface, breathe, and live loudly and proudly.
So, as I feel there is a void from time to time,
I can now see clearly that those holes in my life
have added to
my spirit,
my soul.
The holes have made me whole.

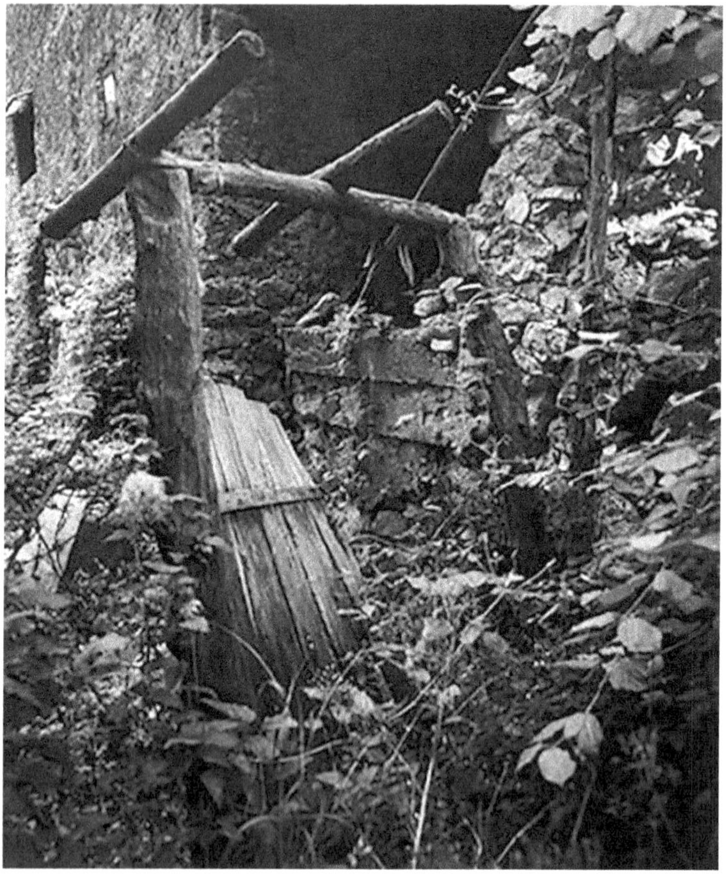

Absence So Present

Your absence is alive, real, raw.

Your absence is so present.

You will always be deep in my heart,

your smile

so warm, long, and strong . . . this nightmare is all wrong.

So many more cherished memories yet to make,

my heart is in permanent break.

Your absence is so present.

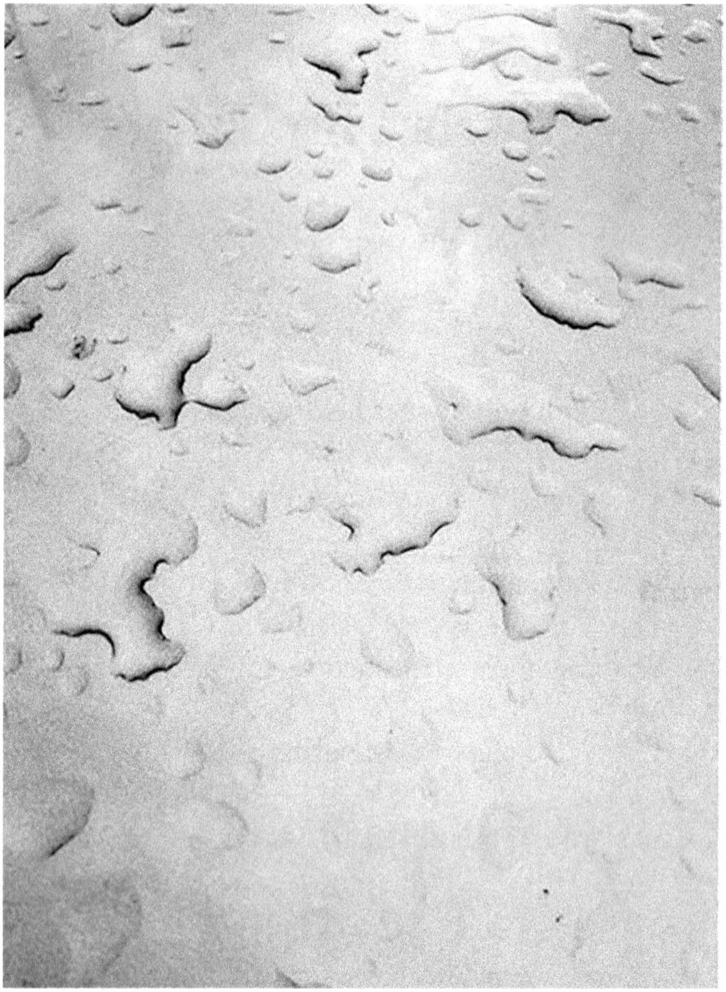

The Best Thing

The best thing for you and me is to
set each other free.

Feelings so intense, words strung together
not making sense.

Kindness has taken a back seat;
cruelty has hold of the wheel.

Forcing a flower to bloom and grow—
no water, warmth, or sun—
the dying has begun.

Poison has replaced honey,
emotions bound and bankrupt.

The best thing for you and me is to
set each other free.

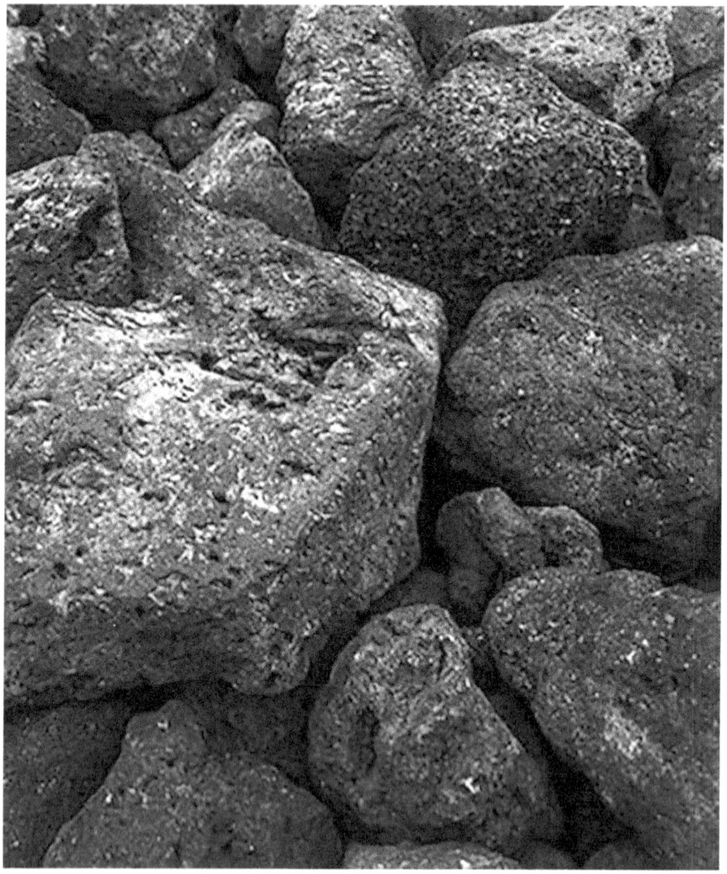

The Shell

I have this outer shell; it protects me well.
No one is fully allowed in.
Some people have tried to break my shell
and never succeeded . . . I hide so well.
Why is it I shelter myself so deep inside?
Maybe to keep a sense of pride.
My shell is like a callus that forms on the skin
hard, tough, and strong.
At times, I wish I could trust enough to
let my outer shell go.
How will I know?
It will take time to let go of the shell.
You will know it's gone
when you know me well.

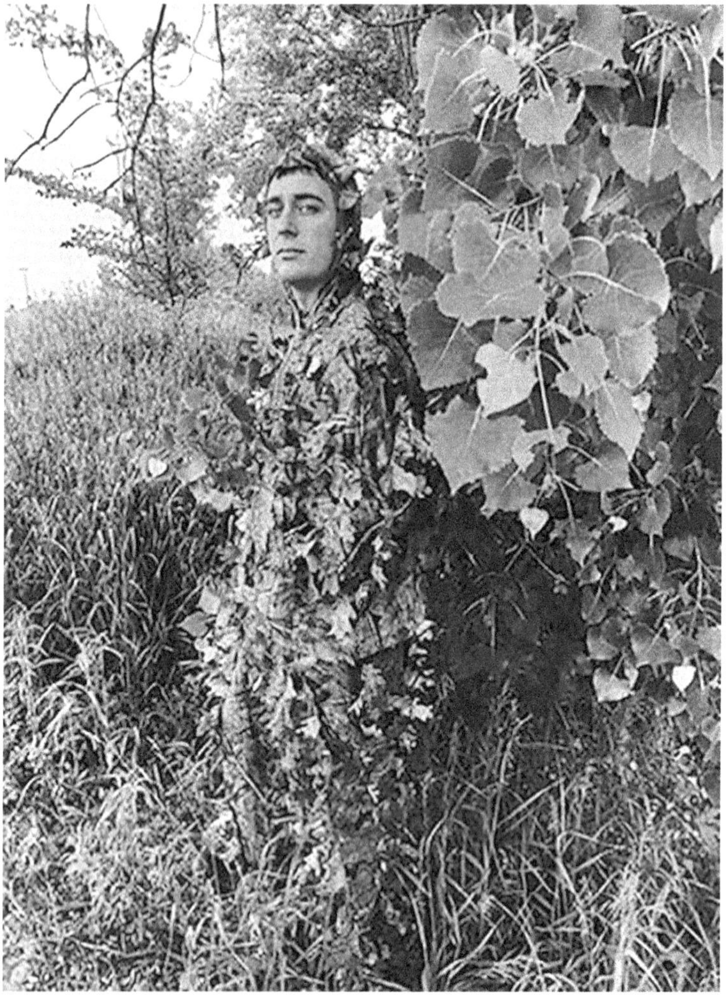

Who's There?

Falsehood comes knocking on my door
disguising itself as the truth . . .
My soul does not answer.

Superficiality disguises itself as reality and
tries to push its way into my room.
There is no space available today
or any day.
My spirit sends it away with a swift kick and
a smile goodbye.

Cruelness tries to force its way into my kind heart.
My eyes see the message; my mind comprehends
the illusion and says, "I want nothing to do with you, nor do
I want to know your ways or follow your crooked path."

Love floats in oh so gently like a feather,
landing on the sea . . .
and opens its arms
out wide to me.

My whole being embraces goodness and realness;
my soul is again nourished.

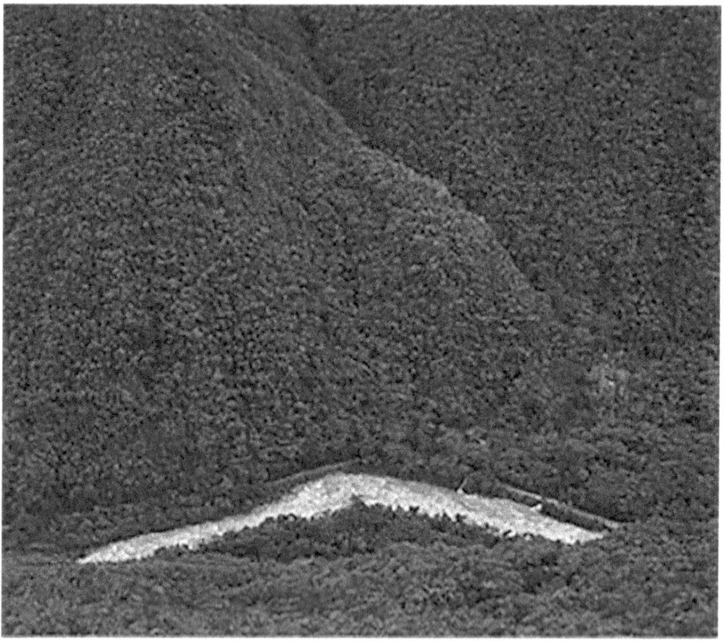

Just for a Day

Just for a day, let no worries clutter my brain.

Just for a day, let me have my way.

Let me have no doubts—
only clarity of thought.

This I ask in a kind way:
Could it happen just for a day?

I would like to hear an abundance of truth, and
honesty to override the lies.

I'd like people to be true when
I look in their eyes.

Can you grant me these wishes and
hear what I say?

I am not asking for forever . . .
just for a day.

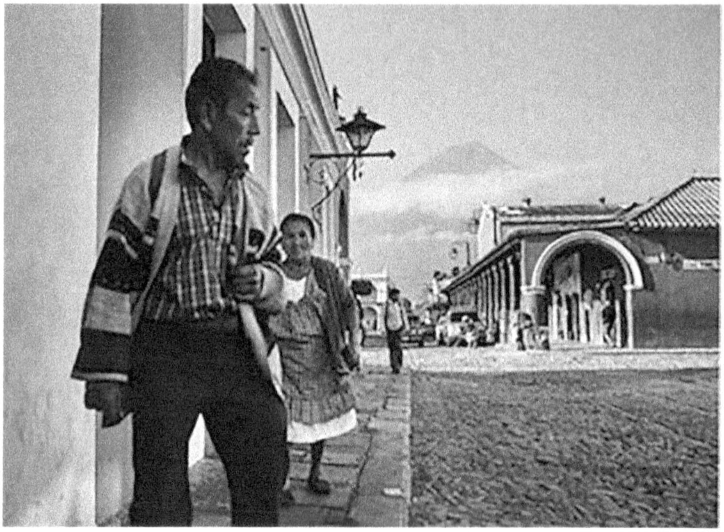

Today

Today, I will do the best I can with what I have.

Today, I will be strong and not crumble to petty criticism.

Today, I will breathe deeply when I feel short of breath.

Today, I will live life as if it was my last; I will not worry about the present, future, or past.

I will live for today the best I can with what I have.

ଈ

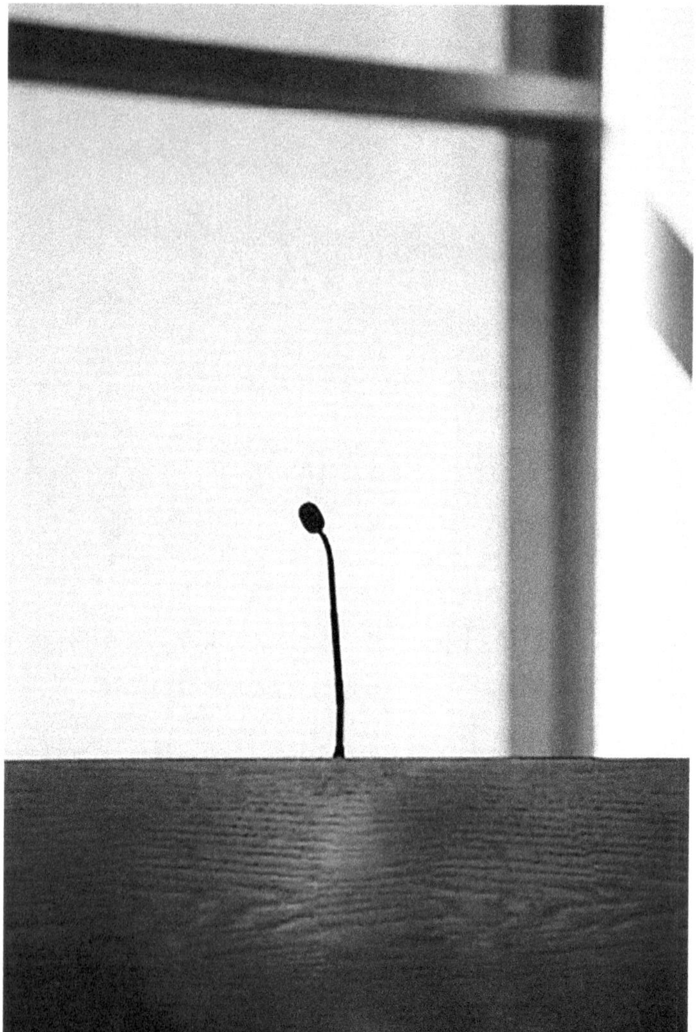

In Awe

*Y*our soft beauty,
your amazing aura—
I am in awe.

Your smile is
luminous, your body
perfect,
ambition, drive, purpose—
I am in awe.

A simple hello and my heart
skips a beat.
Brief when our eyes meet,
I cannot find words to speak . . .
I am in awe.

I am drawn to you like
a moth
to a
flame . . .
just don't want to get burned . . .
I am in awe.

I feel the intense chemistry
oozing, bubbling over—
such passion that would surely
explode if not neatly contained
in my body and brain.

I am in awe,
and
I am in love.

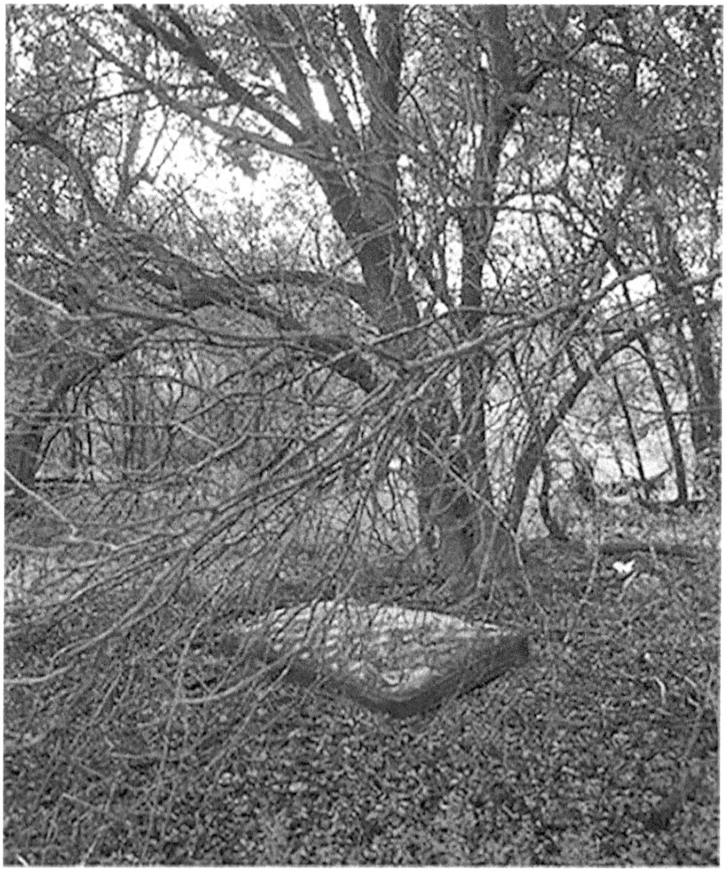

Only So Much

There is only so much I can do;
after that, it's up to you.
I can comfort, be a friend, and
give support;
after that, the ball is in your court.
You need a surrounding of people on your side;
if you choose otherwise, it will shorten your stride.
Be wise in this wild world of life.
If wisdom turns to give in,
it will not be so nice.
Be strong for yourself, and
set your standards high.
Believe in you as I
and others do.

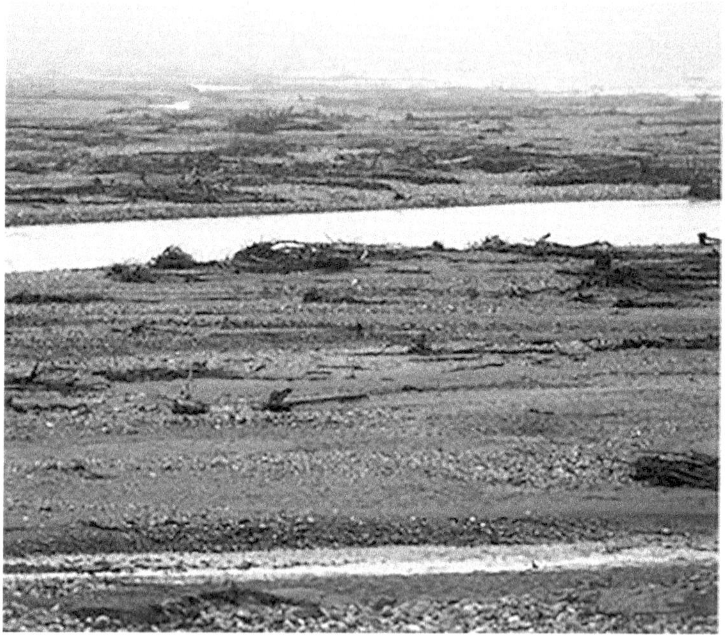

This Life

Transitions; changes; ups and downs;
in-betweens;
waitings; wantings;
deep, dark valleys;
beautiful blue skies;
clouds
floating,
dancing;
winds so soft and gentle,
carrying messages in their silent breeze.

Hard rain pelting down; floods
damage; rageful waters
rain; destruction and nourishment
grow; healing
blossoms, blooms; and trees—
everything changes,
transitions.
Perspective is the key
to
beauty
in
this life.

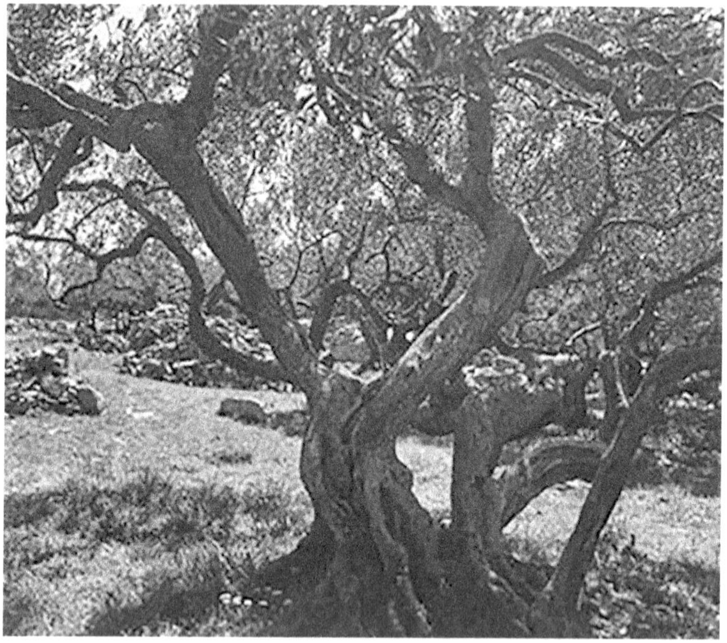

Quietude of My Solitude
By Bruce Bauer

In the quietude of my solitude,
I explore
my latitude and longitude
and meander through the mazes
of my mind.

In the quietude of my solitude,
I question
my -innings: thinking's and unthinking;
speakings, unspeaking; doings, undoings;
and a thousand -innings
to which flesh and unflesh are thereto.

In the quietude of my solitude,
I surmise
the sunrise and moonrise and
the tax rise and the birth rise
and the death rise,
and it's all relative-wise,
so the saged soothsayers say,
and
in the quietude of my solitude,
I return
from Xander to pragmatism and
hedonism and functionalism and narcissism
and infinite -isms refracted through the
prisms of my pancreas.
I return
from Xander and resume
my rote, regurgitation, and restraint.

Photographs:

- vi   North Cascades Mountain Range
- 2   Minneapolis, MN
- 4   Johua Tree NTL Park
- 6   Cerna Valley Romania
- 8   3 States of Aggregation
- 10   New Mexico
- 12   Outskirts of Fez Morroco
- 14   Red Cave Slot Canyon Northern Arizona
- 16   North Star
- 18   Afton Alps Minnesota, MN
- 20   Live Volcano Kona Island Hawaii
- 22   Bad Lands South Dakota
- 24   Fresh Snow in Alaska
- 26   Morning Dew Alaska
- 28   Arches NTL Park Utah
- 30   Rubber Tree in Thailand in Ko Iao Noi Island
- 32   Long Tail Boat in Southern Thailand
- 34   Swirl in Cleveland Ohio
- 36   Buckskin Gulch Canyon Arizona
- 38   Climber in Sandstone Minnesota
- 40   High Dessert of New Mexico
- 42   After Stacking Hay in Romania
- 44   Lightning Bolt Through Plains of North Dakota
- 46   Long Tail Boats Resting at Low Tide Thailand
- 48   High Rise Window Washers Chicago Il
- 50   Pastoral in Transilvania Romania
- 52   Scatered Perspective Mpls, MN
- 54   Palm Trees on Atol Aakarava South Pacific French Polynesia
- 56   A Room with a view, Machu Piciu
- 58   Father with Daughter in Traditional Garb, Big Island, Hawaii
- 60   Downhill slope at whistler mountain BC, Canada
- 62   Street Sign in USVI
- 64   Herb Jar Hong Kong, China
- 66   Cuzco Peru, Kids at the market
- 68   Before the Storm in Alaska
- 70   Guatemala, A couple selling crabs
- 72   Northern Minnesota in the Winter
- 74   Soccer Field in Transylvania Romania
- 76   Outside on a Farm in Mexico City, Mexico
- 78   Signs of Life on a Volcanic Plateau in Hawaii
- 80   Overgrown Household, Romania
- 82   Water on Glass
- 84   Volcanic Rocks in Hawaii
- 86   Camo Suit in New Jersey
- 88   A Bend in the River Urubamba, Peru
- 90   On The Streets of Oaxaca, Mexico
- 92   Speakers Podium MN
- 94   Home Away from Home St Paul MN
- 96   Drift Wood in Alaska
- 98   Olive Trees in Croatia

About the Author

Jami Bauer holds master's degrees in Education and Occupational Therapy. She is a published poet and co-author of Sports for Life, The Fruits of Play and Competition. Jami is a certified tennis professional, personal trainer, and occupational therapist who resides with her wife, Mojca, their dog Daisy and two cats Luna and Brki in Saint Paul, Minnesota.

Adrian Danciu is a cinematographer who started printing photographs in his father's darkroom in Romania when he was young. He is a frequent contributor to Travel Channel's show Bizarre Foods with Andrew Zimmern as well as to commercial, indie film, and still productions. Danciu currently resides in Saint Paul, Minnesota.